Sounds All Around Us

What is Sound?

Charlotte Guillain

www.heinemannlibrary.co.uk
Visit our website to find out more information about Heinemann Library books.

To order:
☎ Phone +44 (0) 1865 888066
🖹 Fax +44 (0) 1865 314091
💻 Visit www.heinemannlibrary.co.uk

Heinemann is an imprint of Capstone Global Library Limited, a company incorporated in England and Wales having its registered office at 7 Pilgrim Street, London, EC4V 6LB – Registered company number: 6695582

"Heinemann" is a registered trademark of Pearson Education Limited, under licence to Capstone Global Library Limited

Edited by Charlotte Guillain, Rebecca Rissman, and Catherine Veitch
Designed by Joanna Hinton-Malivoire
Photo research by Tracy Cummins and Tracey Engel
Originated by Heinemann Library
Printed by South China Printing Company Ltd

ISBN 978 0 431 19335 9 (hardback)
13 12 11 10 09
10 9 8 7 6 5 4 3 2 1

British Library Cataloguing in Publication Data
Guillain, Charlotte
What is sound? - (Sounds all around us)
534
A full catalogue record for this book is available from the British Library.

Acknowledgements
The author and publishers are grateful to the following for permission to reproduce copyright material: age footstock pp. 7 (©Juan Biosca), 11 (©Javier Larrea), 14 (©Demetrio Carrasco/Agency Jon Arnold Images), 23b (©Demetrio Carrasco/Agency Jon Arnold Images); Alamy pp. **4 top left** (©UpperCut Images), 8 (©David Sanger), 9 (©I4images-music-1), 12 (©stock shots by itani), 13 (©stock shots by itani), 16 (©Redferns Music Picture Library), 21 (©David Wall), **23a** (©David Wall), **23c** (©stock shots by itani); Getty Images pp. 6 (©Brett Froomer), 17 (©STOCK4B), 18 (©Gen Nishino), 19 (©Nordic Photos/Lena Johansson); iStockPhoto pp. **4 bottom right** (©Peeter Viisimaa), **4 top right** (©Frank Leung); Photolibrary pp. 5 (©Juniors Bildarchiv), 10 (©Image Source), 15 (©Banana Stock), 20 (©AFLO Royalty Free); Shutterstock **p 4 bottom left** (©devi).

Cover photograph of a road worker digging up tarmac reproduced with permission of Alamy (©Tim Cuff). Back cover photograph of a referee blowing a whistle reproduced with permission of Getty Images (©Stock 4B).

The publishers would like to thank Nancy Harris and Adriana Scalise for their assistance in the preparation of this book.

Every effort has been made to contact copyright holders of any material reproduced in this book. Any omissions will be rectified in subsequent printings if notice is given to the publisher.

Contents

Sounds

There are many different sounds.

We hear different sounds around us every day.

What is sound?

When we play a guitar we hear a sound.

When we play a guitar we make the strings shake.

When we play a drum we hear
a sound.

When we play a drum we make the drum shake.

When we shake something
it vibrates.

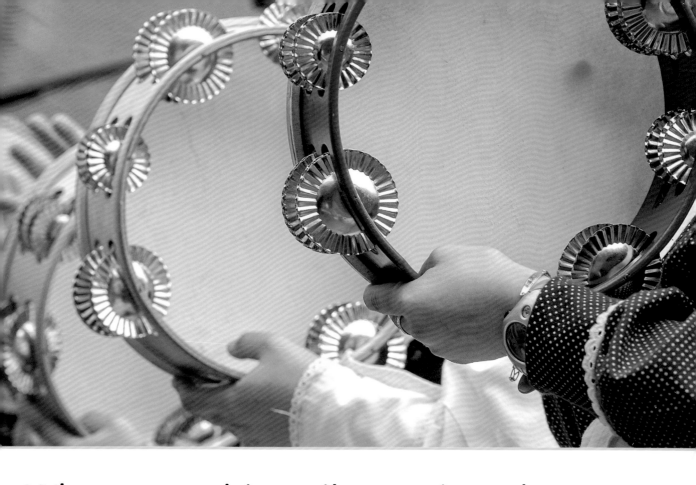

When something vibrates it makes
a sound.

Sound waves

When something vibrates, it makes the air vibrate.

sound wave

When the air vibrates it is called a sound wave.

sound wave

Sound waves move through the air to our ears.

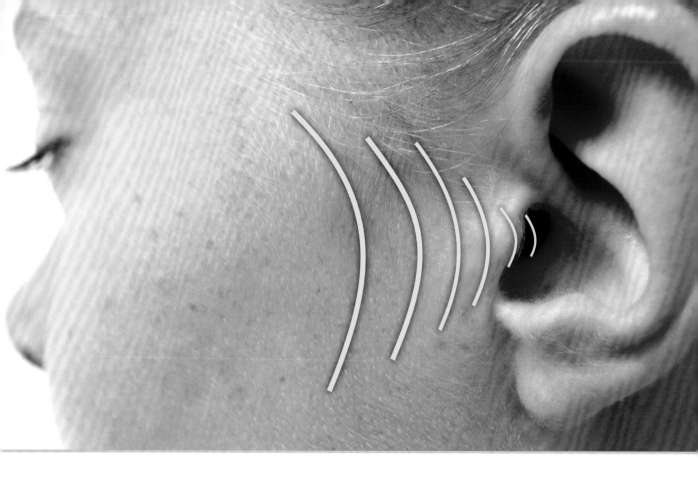

Sound waves move through the air to our ears quickly.

Our ears hear the sound.

Our ears hear the sound quickly.

Sound waves can travel through objects.

Sound waves can travel
through windows.

Echoes

Sound waves can repeat or echo in buildings.

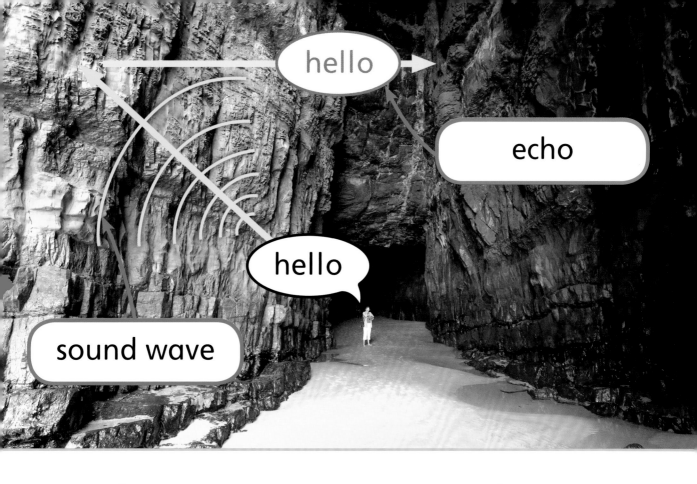

Sound waves can repeat or echo
in caves.

What have you learned?

- When something vibrates it makes a sound.

- When the air vibrates it is called a sound wave.

- We hear an echo when sound waves bounce back to us.

Picture glossary

echo when a sound comes back to you and you hear it again

sound wave when the air shakes very quickly

vibrate shake very quickly

Index

Note to parents and teachers
Before reading
Tell the children that when something vibrates, it makes a sound. Hold up a musical triangle and play it. Ask the children to look at how the triangle vibrates when it is hit. Tell the children that when the triangle vibrates it makes the air vibrate, and creates a sound wave. Tell the children that when sound waves bounce back to us we hear an echo. Explain that an echo is when we hear the same sound again.

After reading
Try bouncing sound in this fun experiment. You will need one plate, several books, a ticking watch, a long cardboard tube, and two children. Build two piles of books that are the same height. Then lay the tube on the books. Ask child A to hold the watch to their ear. Instruct them to listen carefully to the ticking watch. Next, ask child B to hold the watch at the far end of the tube. Tell child A to listen through the tube. Can they hear the watch? Ask child B to next hold a plate at the far end of the tube, behind the watch. Can child A hear the watch now? Discuss what has happened with the children. Explain that when the plate is put at the end of the tube, it makes the sound bounce back and forth creating an echo.

BETTWS

7.8.18